Editor in Chief
Ina Massler Levin, M.A.

Editor
Eric Migliaccio

Contributing Editor
Sarah Smith

Creative Director
Karen J. Goldfluss, M.S. Ed.

Cover Design
Tony Carrillo / Marilyn Goldberg

Teacher Created Resources
12621 Western Avenue
Garden Grove, CA 92841
www.teachercreated.com

ISBN: 978-1-4206-5928-3

Reprinted, 2026
Made in U.S.A.

This book belongs to

____

Ready·Set·Learn

Get Ready to Learn!

Get ready, get set, and go! Boost your child's learning with this exciting series of books. Geared to help children practice and master many needed skills, the *Ready·Set·Learn* books are bursting with 64 pages of learning fun. Use these books for . . .

- enrichment
- skills reinforcement
- extra practice

With their smaller size, the *Ready·Set·Learn* books fit easily in children's hands, backpacks, and book bags. All your child needs to get started are pencils, crayons, and colored pencils.

A full sheet of colorful stickers is included. Use these stickers for . . .

- decorating pages
- rewarding outstanding effort
- keeping track of completed pages

Celebrate your child's progress by using these stickers on the reward chart located on the inside cover. The blue-ribbon sticker fits perfectly on the certificate on page 64.

With *Ready·Set·Learn* and a little encouragement, your child will be on the fast track to learning fun!

Multiplication #1

Directions: Add each of these problems. Look for the pattern.

1. $$\begin{array}{r} 5 \\ 5 \\ +\ 5 \\ \hline \end{array}$$

2. $$\begin{array}{r} 4 \\ 4 \\ +\ 4 \\ \hline \end{array}$$

3. $$\begin{array}{r} 2 \\ 2 \\ 2 \\ +\ 2 \\ \hline \end{array}$$

4. $$\begin{array}{r} 6 \\ 6 \\ 6 \\ +\ 6 \\ \hline \end{array}$$

5. 8 + 8 + 8 = ____

6. 9 + 9 + 9 = ____

7. $$\begin{array}{r} 2 \\ 2 \\ 2 \\ 2 \\ +\ 2 \\ \hline \end{array}$$

8. $$\begin{array}{r} 3 \\ 3 \\ 3 \\ 3 \\ 3 \\ +\ 3 \\ \hline \end{array}$$

9. $$\begin{array}{r} 1 \\ 1 \\ 1 \\ 1 \\ 1 \\ 1 \\ +\ 1 \\ \hline \end{array}$$

10. $$\begin{array}{r} 7 \\ 7 \\ 7 \\ 7 \\ +\ 7 \\ \hline \end{array}$$

11. 4 + 4 + 4 + 4 + 4 = ____

12. 3 + 3 + 3 + 3 + 3 = ____

Multiplication #2

Directions: Solve and draw.

Example: 4 groups of cars with 3 in each group.

1. 5 groups of trees with 2 in each group.

2. 3 groups of bananas with 3 in each group.

3. 2 groups of stars with 4 in each group.

4. 3 groups of checkmarks with 4 in each group.

Directions: Use the drawing to fill in the blanks.

5. ______ groups of ______

6. ______ groups of ______

Multiplication #3

Directions: Use the pictures to make your own addition and multiplication problems.

1.

3 + 3 + 3 = □ *or* □ x □ = □

2.

2 + 2 + 2 + 2 = □ *or* □ x □ = □

3.

4 + 4 + 4 = □ *or* □ x □ = □

4.

5 + 5 = □ *or* □ x □ = □

Multiplication #4

Directions: Alexis is wild about making math problems with arrays. Help her make multiplication facts for each array in the bottom of each cone.

Cone 1

Cone 2

Cone 3

Cone 4

Multiplication #5

Directions: Fill in the blank on each multiplication problem.

1. 9 x ____ = 9

2. 1 x ____ = 4

3. 7 x ____ = 7

4. 1 x 8 = ____

5. 3 x 1 = ____

6. 2 x 1 = ____

7. 1 x 1 = ____

8. 1 x ____ = 1

9. 11 x 1 = ____

Multiplication #6

Directions: Answer these multiplication problems as fast as you can.

1. 1 x 2 = ☐ **2.** 4 x 2 = ☐ **3.** 10 x 2 = ☐

4. 2 x 2 = ☐ **5.** 5 x 2 = ☐ **6.** 11 x 2 = ☐

7. 3 x 2 = ☐ **8.** 6 x 2 = ☐ **9.** 12 x 2 = ☐

10. 7 x 2 = ☐

11. 8 x 2 = ☐

12. 9 x 2 = ☐

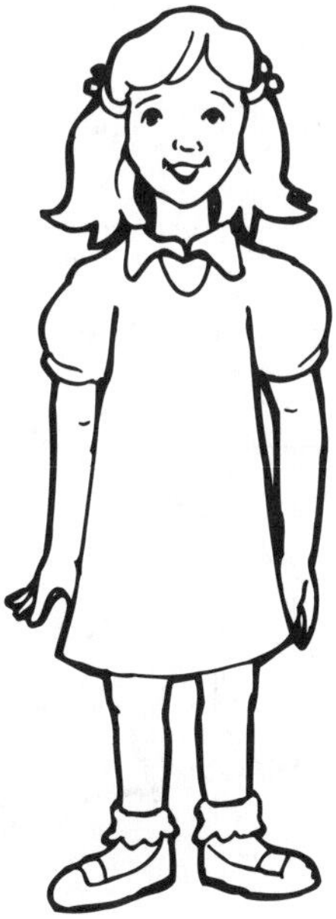

Multiplication #7

Directions: Practice multiplying by three. Color only the boxes that have a correct answer.

4 x 3 = 11	4 x 3 = 12	3 x 1 = 3	3 x 9 = 27	3 x 8 = 29	3 x 2 = 9
3 x 1 = 0	3 x 4 = 9	3 x 2 = 0	3 x 1 = 3	3 x 11 = 11	3 x 12 = 33
2 x 3 = 18	3 x 8 = 24	3 x 12 = 36	7 x 3 = 21	6 x 3 = 12	3 x 1 = 4
9 x 3 = 17	3 x 0 = 3	2 x 3 = 8	3 x 9 = 27	3 x 10 = 40	7 x 3 = 29
3 x 3 = 11	3 x 6 = 18	3 x 2 = 6	7 x 3 = 21	3 x 3 = 36	3 x 1 = 6
3 x 0 = 30	5 x 3 = 14	3 x 7 = 24	9 x 3 = 17	3 x 4 = 7	6 x 3 = 9

Multiplication #8

Directions: Circle the number of triangles that match the equation. Then count the dots inside each triangle to solve the equations. The first one has been done for you.

1. 4 groups of 3 = 12 4 x 3 = 12

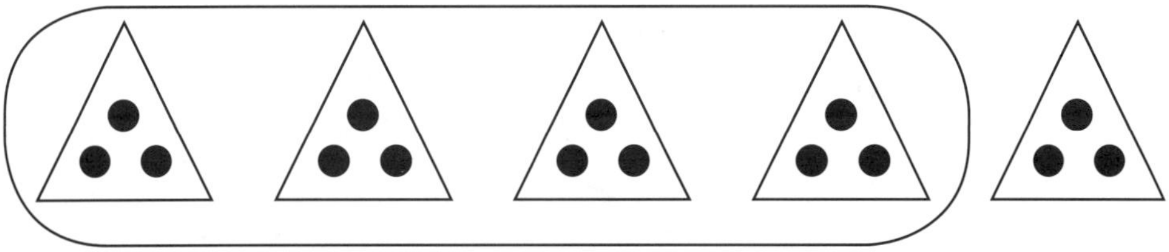

2. 6 groups of 3 = 6 x 3 = ________

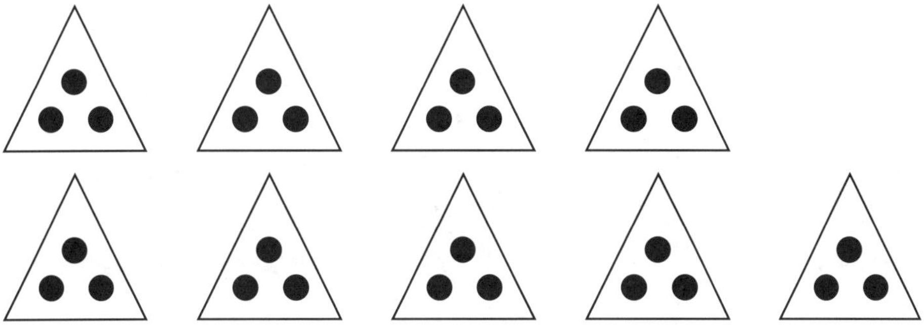

3. 9 groups of 3 = 9 x 3 = ________

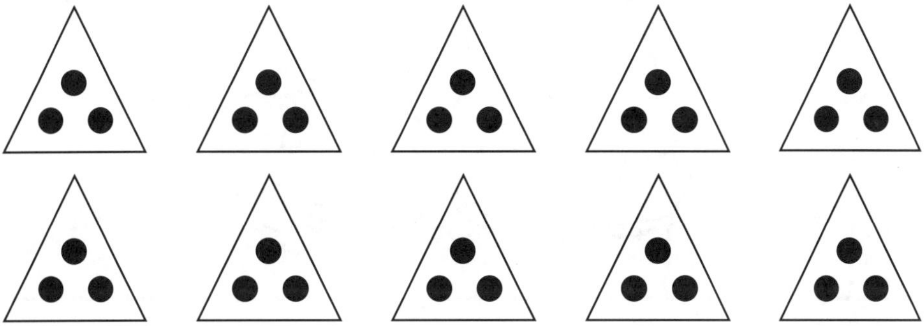

Multiplication #9

Directions: Solve each multiplication problem. Color the puzzle.

2 = red	4 = yellow	6 = green	8 = blue	10 = orange	12 = purple

Multiplication #10

Directions: Answer each problem.

1.

4 x 0 = ☐

4 x 7 = ☐

1 x 4 = ☐

4 x 12 = ☐

2.

11 x 4 = ☐

3 x 4 = ☐

8 x 4 = ☐

4 x 6 = ☐

3.

2 x 4 = ☐

5 x 4 = ☐

4 x 9 = ☐

10 x 4 = ☐

4.

4 x 1 = ☐

4 x 8 = ☐

4 x 2 = ☐

7 x 4 = ☐

Multiplication #11

Directions: Find the answer to each multiplication problem. Use the five points on each star to help you find the answer.

1. 5 x 5 = ______ 

2. 7 x 5 = ______ 

3. 1 x 5 = ______ 

4. 2 x 5 = ______ 

5. 8 x 5 = ______ 

Bonus: How many total points are on the 10 stars? Write an equation to help you find the answer.

__________ x __________ = __________

Multiplication #12

Directions: Solve each multiplication problem. Write the letter that goes with the answer for each problem on the line at the bottom of the page.

5	10	15	20	25	30	35	40	45	50	55
A	C	I	L	M	N	O	P	T	U	Y

1. $2 \times 5 = \square$

2. $5 \times 1 = \square$

3. $6 \times 5 = \square$

4. $5 \times 11 = \square$

5. $5 \times 7 = \square$

6. $10 \times 5 = \square$

7. $5 \times 5 = \square$

8. $5 \times 10 = \square$

9. $5 \times 4 = \square$

10. $5 \times 9 = \square$

11. $3 \times 5 = \square$

12. $8 \times 5 = \square$

13. $4 \times 5 = \square$

14. $11 \times 5 = \square$

___ ___ ___   ___ ___ ___   ___ ___ ___ ___ ___ ___ ___ ___ ?

1 2 3   4 5 6   7 8 9 10 11 12 13 14

Multiplication #13

Directions: Look at each set of problems. Circle the sets. Then write the product (answer) for the 2 factors.

1. 3 x 2 = ______ 

2. 5 x 2 = ______ 

3. 1 x 2 = ______ 

4. 2 x 2 = ______ 

5. 4 x 2 = ______ 

6. 7 x 2 = ______ 

7. 6 x 2 = ______ 

8. 2 x 9 = ______ 

Multiplication #14

Directions: Solve these problems. Write your answers on the lines.

1. 6 x 1 = ______

2. 6 x 2 = ______

3. 6 x 4 = ______

4. 5 x 6 = ______

5. 3 x 6 = ______

6. 6 x 9 = ______

7. 6 x 6 = ______

8. 6 x 10 = ______

9. 8 x 6 = ______

10. 6 x 7 = ______

Directions: Draw lines to match the equations to their answers.

6 x 2	**24**	6 x 9
6 x 4	**48**	4 x 6
9 x 6	**12**	6 x 8
8 x 6	**54**	2 x 6

Ready·Set·Learn

Multiplication #15

Directions: Solve these problems. Write your answers on the lines.

1. 7 x 1 = ______

2. 7 x 2 = ______

3. 7 x 4 = ______

4. 5 x 7 = ______

5. 3 x 7 = ______

6. 7 x 9 = ______

7. 7 x 6 = ______

8. 7 x 10 = ______

9. 8 x 7 = ______

10. 6 x 7 = ______

Directions: Draw lines to match the equations to their answers.

7 x 2	**56**	7 x 9
7 x 4	**28**	4 x 7
9 x 7	**63**	7 x 8
8 x 7	**14**	2 x 7

Multiplication #16

Directions: Out on the beat at 7 A.M., police officers Betty and Bernice pick up a trail. A brazen thief has stolen multiples of seven! Fortunately, the thief has dropped some along the way. So follow the trail until you exit the city block—and catch the thief!

	↓							49	
	7	21	49	70	77	50	14	56	
49	15				28			70	
	35	84	42	48	35	70	84	23	77
				20			21		70
←	14	63	56	42			14		56
	17			35	29	22	35	42	55
	77			56		48		49	70
	35	27	37	77	35	28			77
			48			14	7	14	28

Multiplication #17

Directions: Solve these problems.

1. 3 x 8	**2.** 2 x 8	**3.** 4 x 8	**4.** 5 x 8
5. 1 x 7	**6.** 10 x 7	**7.** 4 x 7	**8.** 2 x 6
9. 3 x 6	**10.** 5 x 6	**11.** 5 x 9	**12.** 0 x 9
13. 1 x 9	**14.** 2 x 9	**15.** 5 x 8	**16.** 10 x 6

Multiplication #18

Directions: Follow the path from home to school to get you through the multiplication review.

Multiplication #19

Directions: Draw pictures and complete.

1. Five girls had three lollipops each. How many lollipops altogether? _______ x ______ = ______ lollipops
2. One caterpillar had ten legs. How many legs altogether? _______ x ______ = ______ legs
3. Four boys each had two dollars. How much did they have altogether? _______ x ______ = ______ dollars
4. There are four sharks. Each shark has eight teeth. How many teeth altogether? _______ x ______ = ______ teeth
5. There were two trees. Each tree had seven apples on it. How many apples altogether? _______ x ______ = ______ apples

Multiplication #20

Directions: Solve and write your answers in the boxes.

1. 8 x □ 80	**2.** 8 x 0 □	**3.** 8 x □ 24	**4.** 8 x □ 48
5. 8 x □ 40	**6.** 8 x 8 6□	**7.** □ x 1 8	**8.** 8 x □ 56
9. 8 x 2 □6	**10.** 8 x □ 72	**11.** 8 x 4 3□	**12.** 8 x □ 88

Multiplication #21

Directions: Solve these problems.

1. 9 x 4	**2.** 7 x 6	**3.** 4 x 4	**4.** 0 x 9
5. 9 x 8	**6.** 7 x 8	**7.** 6 x 1	**8.** 4 x 6
9. 5 x 4	**10.** 3 x 8	**11.** 5 x 9	**12.** 8 x 8
13. 5 x 8	**14.** 3 x 7	**15.** 9 x 7	**16.** 8 x 7

Ready·Set·Learn

Multiplication #22

Directions: Color the path to show multiples of 9. Start at the number 9 and finish at the number 135.

9	18	24	33	49
12	27	19	44	51
45	36	28	37	67
54	63	72	81	91
61	111	99	90	97
77	107	108	115	122
84	133	117	126	135

Ready·Set·Learn

Multiplication #23

Directions: Fill in the missing factors.

1. 10 x _____ = 50

2. 9 x _____ = 18

3. 5 x _____ = 20

4. 5 x _____ = 40

5. _____ x 8 = 80

6. 7 x _____ = 35

7. 6 x _____ = 36

8. 8 x _____ = 32

9. _____ x 6 = 60

10. _____ x 7 = 42

11. _____ x 9 = 81

12. 4 x _____ = 12

13. 2 x _____ = 18

14. _____ x 7 = 49

15. _____ x 8 = 48

16. _____ x 6 = 48

17. 10 x _____ = 40

18. 9 x _____ = 72

19. 3 x _____ = 27

20. 6 x _____ = 24

21. _____ x 5 = 50

22. 8 x _____ = 56

23. _____ x 9 = 54

24. 6 x _____ = 54

25. _____ x 3 = 21

26. 7 x _____ = 56

27. _____ x 9 = 36

Multiplication #24

Directions: Complete each chart to find the multiples of 6, 7, 8, and 9. The first answer has been given.

1.

x	7	4	2	5	3	8	6	9
6	42							

2.

x	7	4	2	5	3	8	6	9
7								

3.

x	7	4	2	5	3	8	6	9
8								

4.

x	7	4	2	5	3	8	6	9
9								

Multiplication #25

Directions: Color the factors for 18 blue and the remaining numbers black.

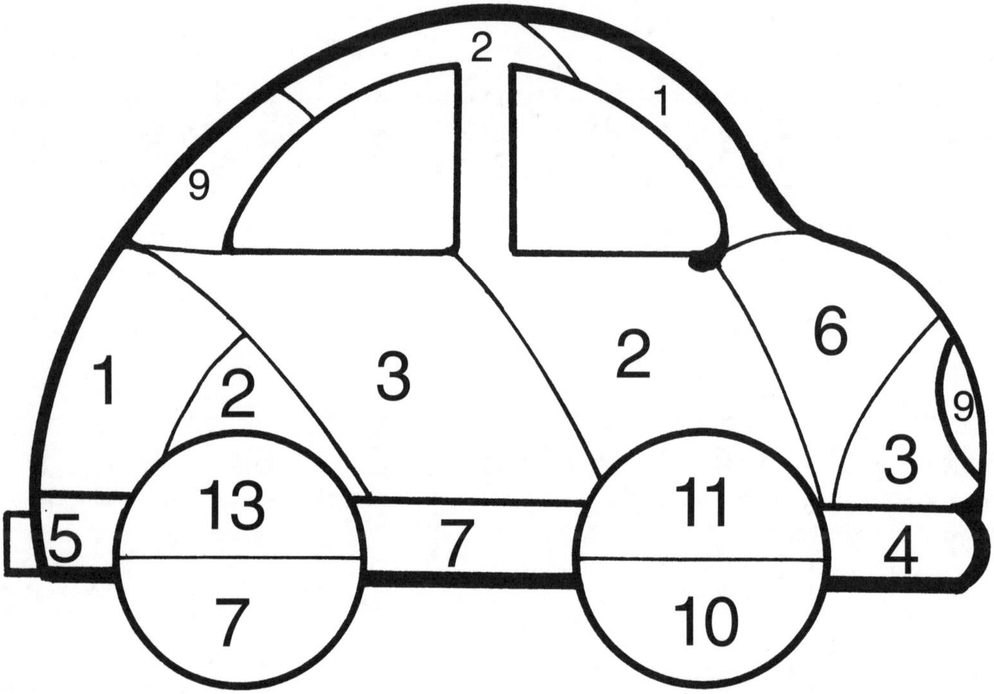

Directions: Write the factors for each number.

1. 4: ______________________________

2. 6: ______________________________

3. 9: ______________________________

4. 10: ______________________________

5. 15: ______________________________

Multiplication #26

Directions: Solve the math problems below. Match each answer to a letter from the chart. Put the letters in the boxes. The letters should spell out the answer to the question below.

O = 36	**I** = 81	**W** = 24	**D** = 35
R = 54	**L** = 49	**N** = 72	**S** = 42

1. 6 x 4 = ________ ☐
2. 12 x 3 = ________ ☐
3. 9 x 4 = ________ ☐
4. 7 x 5 = ________ ☐
5. 9 x 6 = ________ ☐
6. 4 x 9 = ________ ☐
7. 12 x 2 = ________ ☐
8. 8 x 3 = ________ ☐
9. 9 x 9 = ________ ☐
10. 7 x 7 = ________ ☐
11. 6 x 7 = ________ ☐
12. 6 x 6 = ________ ☐
13. 9 x 8 = ________ ☐

Bonus: Whose face was on the $100,000 bill?

Multiplication #27

Directions: Write the number word for each answer below. Then use your answers to fill in the crossword puzzle.

Across

2. 6 x 1 = ________

5. 9 x 1 = ________

6. 3 x 4 = ________

7. 7 x 2 = ________

Down

1. 8 x 2 = ________

3. 3 x 5 = ________

4. 0 x 8 = ________

6. 2 x 5 = ________

Multiplication #28

Directions: Solve the problems and write the number word for each answer. Circle those number words in the puzzle below.

E	Z	Q	F	C	Z	G	Y	T	H
I	W	S	F	I	F	T	Y	W	U
I	W	E	L	N	R	K	L	E	N
U	T	V	T	O	I	O	Y	L	D
Y	H	E	F	G	K	N	G	V	R
X	I	N	G	O	U	T	E	E	E
O	R	T	C	A	H	S	G	A	D
S	T	Y	V	G	Y	G	Q	D	M
Z	Y	K	I	T	W	E	N	T	Y
O	U	E	I	G	H	T	E	E	N

1. 8 x 1 = ________

2. 5 x 4 = ________

3. 6 x 5 = ________

4. 6 x 3 = ________

5. 2 x 6 = ________

6. 8 x 5 = ________

7. 3 x 3 = ________

8. 7 x 10 = ________

9. 10 x 5 = ________

10. 10 x 10 = ________

Multiplication #29

Directions: Read each word problem and solve it using multiplication.

1. Sue needs buttons for an art project she is doing with her children. She bought 4 packages of buttons. Each package has 12 buttons. How many buttons did Sue buy in all?

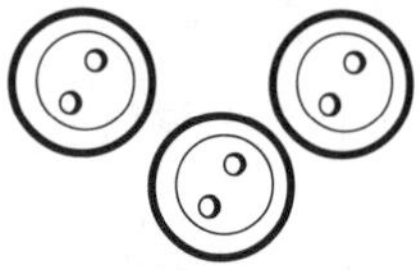

________ buttons

2. Agnes bought 3 bags of carrots from the store. Each bag held 14 carrots. How many total carrots did Agnes buy?

________ carrots

3. Betty placed 9 pictures on each of the 4 shelves in her living room. How many total pictures does Betty have on the shelves? *(Circle the correct letter.)*

A. 5 B. 14 C. 36 D. 45

4. Jefferson saw 8 cows at his uncle's farm. How many legs do 8 cows have altogether?

__________ legs

5. Mandy is buying paintbrushes for her art class. She buys 5 packages of paintbrushes with 4 paintbrushes in each package. How many total paintbrushes did Mandy buy?

A. 15 B. 9 C. 20 D. 24

Ready·Set·Learn

Multiplication #30

Directions: Solve these problems.

1. 11 x 10	**2.** 12 x 10	**3.** 8 x 12	**4.** 11 x 12
5. 11 x 3	**6.** 9 x 11	**7.** 6 x 12	**8.** 10 x 12
9. 6 x 11	**10.** 4 x 12	**11.** 12 x 9	**12.** 11 x 8
13. 7 x 11	**14.** 3 x 12	**15.** 12 x 11	**16.** 7 x 12

Multiplication #31

Directions: Answer each word problem and write the multiplication problem.

1. Joanie has 13 marble bags. Inside each bag, there are 6 marbles. How many marbles does Joanie have in all?

Joanie has __________ marbles in all.

2. Mary has 3 dogs. Each dog eats 5 biscuits a day. How many dog biscuits do Mary's dogs eat in a day?

Mary's dogs eat __________ biscuits in a day.

3. Each basket holds 13 apples. How many apples will the 8 baskets hold in all?

The 8 baskets will hold __________ apples in all.

4. Katie has 4 books. If she reads 16 pages in each book every day, how many pages does Katie read in a day.

Katie reads __________ pages in a day.

5. Sasha is having a birthday party. She invited 17 friends to the party. If each friend gets 3 cupcakes, how many cupcakes does Sasha need to buy?

Sasha needs to buy __________ cupcakes.

Multiplication #32

Directions: Solve these problems. The first one has been done for you.

1. 12 x 4 = 48	**2.** 14 x 2	**3.** 13 x 3	**4.** 21 x 3
5. 44 x 2	**6.** 22 x 4	**7.** 34 x 2	**8.** 50 x 8
9. 54 x 2	**10.** 43 x 2	**11.** 33 x 3	**12.** 71 x 9
13. 70 x 9	**14.** 90 x 7	**15.** 50 x 6	**16.** 60 x 8

Multiplication #33

Directions: Solve each multiplication problem. Use the answers and the letters in each star to decode the secret message.

I	15 x 2
T	73 x 1
A	11 x 6
S	33 x 3
S	44 x 1
A	15 x 1
H	12 x 2
L	65 x 0
I	23 x 1
N	11 x 8
E	57 x 1
K	30 x 3
R	36 x 1
E	41 x 2

Secret Message:

___	___	___	___	___		___	___	___	___		___		___	___	___	___!
99	24	30	88	82		0	23	90	57		66		44	73	15	36

Ready·Set·Learn

Multiplication #34

Directions: Solve these problems. The first one has been done for you.

1. 33 x 3 = 99	2. 15 x 2	3. 23 x 3	4. 41 x 6
5. 34 x 2	6. 25 x 3	7. 32 x 4	8. 25 x 5
9. 24 x 2	10. 22 x 5	11. 18 x 5	12. 27 x 5
13. 36 x 3	14. 44 x 5	15. 33 x 8	16. 66 x 2

Multiplication #35

Directions: Solve each multiplication problem. Write each product in the number puzzle. The first one has been done for you.

Across

4. 19 x 4 = 76

6. 67 x 2 = ____________

8. 22 x 8 = ____________

9. 73 x 5 = ____________

11. 86 x 7 = ____________

13. 79 x 6 = ____________

15. 42 x 9 = ____________

16. 98 x 6 = ____________

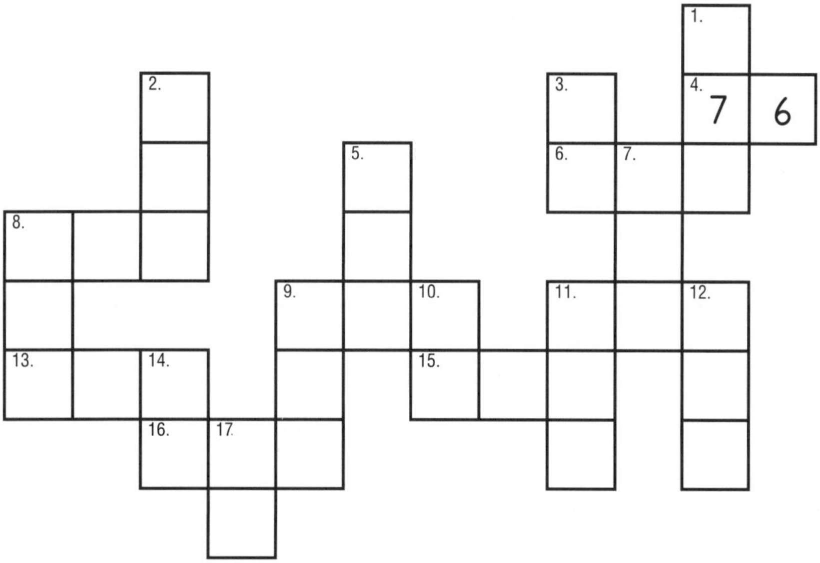

Down

1. 86 x 9 = ____________

2. 28 x 7 = ____________

3. 31 x 1 = ____________

5. 24 x 9 = ____________

7. 64 x 5 = ____________

8. 38 x 3 = ____________

9. 46 x 8 = ____________

10. 53 x 1 = ____________

11. 85 x 8 = ____________

12. 74 x 3 = ____________

14. 15 x 3 = ____________

17. 89 x 1 = ____________

Multiplication #36

Directions: Compute the answer to each problem by multiplying two of the factors. Then multiply that product by the third factor. The first one has been done for you.

1. 2 x 4 x 3 = 2 x 4 = 8 8 x 3 = 24 Answer: 24	**2.** 3 x 4 x 2 = 3 x 4 = _____ 12 x 2 = _____ Answer: _______	**3.** 4 x 2 x 3 = 4 x 2 = _____ 8 x 3 = _____ Answer: _______
4. 3 x 6 x 2 = Answer: _______	**5.** 6 x 2 x 3 = Answer: _______	**6.** 2 x 3 x 6 = Answer: _______
7. 5 x 6 x 4 = Answer: _______	**8.** 6 x 5 x 4 = Answer: _______	**9.** 4 x 5 x 6 = Answer: _______
10. 7 x 3 x 5 = Answer: _______	**11.** 3 x 5 x 7 = Answer: _______	**12.** 5 x 7 x 3 = Answer: _______

Multiplication #37

Directions: Solve these problems. The first one has been done for you.

1. 63 x 4 = 252	**2.** 75 x 6	**3.** 93 x 7	**4.** 47 x 6
5. 95 x 8	**6.** 87 x 5	**7.** 79 x 3	**8.** 85 x 7
9. 67 x 9	**10.** 92 x 4	**11.** 78 x 9	**12.** 99 x 8
13. 57 x 8	**14.** 33 x 7	**15.** 19 x 3	**16.** 56 x 7

Multiplication #38

Directions: Solve these problems.

1. 12 × 10 = 00 + 120 = 120	**2.** 32 × 10	**3.** 23 × 10	**4.** 11 × 10
5. 14 × 10	**6.** 33 × 10	**7.** 18 × 10	**8.** 20 × 10
9. 30 × 10	**10.** 70 × 10	**11.** 24 × 10	**12.** 31 × 10
13. 41 × 10	**14.** 44 × 10	**15.** 25 × 10	**16.** 37 × 10

Multiplication #39

Directions: Solve each trivia problem.

1. Number of months in one year x number of days in one week

Answer: ____________

2. Number of holes in a donut x number of holes in a piece of binder paper

Answer: ____________

3. Number of peanuts in a shell x number of eggs in a dozen

Answer: ____________

4. A set of triplets x total number of fingers on two hands

Answer: ____________

5. Number of toes on both feet x number of fingers on both hands

Answer: ____________

Multiplication #40

Directions: Solve each problem and answer each question.

1.

$$\begin{array}{r} 211 \\ \times\ \ 4 \\ \hline \end{array}$$

In the answer, what number is in the *tens* place?

____

2.

$$\begin{array}{r} 320 \\ \times\ \ 3 \\ \hline \end{array}$$

In the answer, what number is in the *hundreds* place?

____

3.

$$\begin{array}{r} 107 \\ \times\ \ 1 \\ \hline \end{array}$$

In the answer, what number is in the *ones* place?

____

4.

$$\begin{array}{r} 111 \\ \times\ \ 5 \\ \hline \end{array}$$

In the answer, what number is in the *tens* place?

____

5.

$$\begin{array}{r} 848 \\ \times\ \ 1 \\ \hline \end{array}$$

In the answer, what number is in the *hundreds* place?

____

6.

$$\begin{array}{r} 313 \\ \times\ \ 3 \\ \hline \end{array}$$

In the answer, what number is in the *ones* place?

____

Multiplication #41

Directions: Complete this multiplication chart.

x	0	1	2	3	4	5	6	7	8	9	10
0	0					0					0
1		1				5				9	
2			4			10			16		
3				9		15		21			
4					16	20	24				
5	0	5	10	15	20	25	30	35	40	45	50
6					24	30	36				
7				21		35		49			
8			16			40			64		
9		9				45				81	
10	0					50					100

Directions: Use the > (greater than), < (less than), or = (same as) symbols.

1. 5 x 1 ◯ 10 x 2

2. 4 x 7 ◯ 9 x 5

3. 6 x 9 ◯ 7 x 9

4. 3 x 1 ◯ 8 x 3

5. 6 x 2 ◯ 2 x 6

6. 8 x 7 ◯ 4 x 1

Multiplication #42

Directions: Use the > (greater than), < (less than), or = (same as) symbols.

1. 5 x 1 ◯ 1 x 2

2. 3 x 1 ◯ 8 x 3

3. 4 x 7 ◯ 9 x 5

4. 6 x 2 ◯ 2 x 6

5. 6 x 9 ◯ 7 x 9

6. 8 x 7 ◯ 4 x 1

7. 4 x 9 ◯ 5 x 8

8. 8 x 3 ◯ 4 x 6

9. 6 x 5 ◯ 7 x 4

10. 5 x 7 ◯ 4 x 8

Directions: Fill in a number that makes each number sentence true.

11. 6 x 6 > 9 x ______

12. 5 x 9 < 8 x ______

13. 7 x 7 > 4 x ______

14. 3 x 8 = 6 x ______

15. 12 x 12 < 10 x ______

Multiplication #43

Directions: Calculate the area of these rectangles. The first one has been started for you.

1.

7 ft.

10 ft.

Area = 7 x 10 = ________ sq. ft.

2.

9 yd.

8 yd.

Area = ________ sq. yd.

3.

9 m

12 m

Area = ________ sq. m

4.

12 in.

15 in.

Area = ________ sq. in.

5.

17 m

19 m

Area = ________ sq. m

6.

11 ft.

13 ft.

Area = ________ sq. ft.

Multiplication #44

Directions: Solve the multiplications problems. Then draw a line from a kite to its matching kite ribbon.

1. $3,333 \times 3$

7. $7,108 \times 1$

2. $4,103 \times 2$

6. $2,304 \times 2$

3. $1,261 \times 1$

4. $3,400 \times 0$

5. $2,122 \times 4$

Kite ribbons: **8,206**, **1,261**, **7,108**, **8,488**, **4,608**, **0**, **9,999**

Multiplication #45

Step 1: Multiply the factors in the ones column (4 x 6 = 24 or 2 tens and 4 ones). Record the 4 ones in the ones column and regroup the 2 tens to the tens column.	**Step 2:** Move to the tens column. Multiply the factors 6 x 0 and add the 2 tens (6 x 0 = 0 + 2 = 2 tens). Record the 2 tens.	**Step 3:** Move to the hundreds column. Multiply 6 x 1 and record the answer.
[2] 104 x 6 4 = 24	[2] 104 x 6 24	[2] 104 x 6 624

Directions: Solve each multiplication problem.

1. □
   106
   x 8

2. □
   108
   x 7

3. □
   129
   x 2

4. □
   1,114
   x 7

5. □
   102
   x 9

6. □
   2,328
   x 3

7. □
   107
   x 9

8. □
   215
   x 2

Ready·Set·Learn

Multiplication #46

Directions: Solve each multiplication problem.

1. $\begin{array}{r} 123 \\ \times\ 3 \\ \hline \end{array}$

2. $\begin{array}{r} 214 \\ \times\ 2 \\ \hline \end{array}$

3. $\begin{array}{r} 324 \\ \times\ 2 \\ \hline \end{array}$

4. $\begin{array}{r} 232 \\ \times\ 3 \\ \hline \end{array}$

5. $\begin{array}{r} 333 \\ \times\ 3 \\ \hline \end{array}$

6. $\begin{array}{r} 642 \\ \times\ 2 \\ \hline \end{array}$

7. $\begin{array}{r} 922 \\ \times\ 3 \\ \hline \end{array}$

8. $\begin{array}{r} 832 \\ \times\ 3 \\ \hline \end{array}$

Directions: Try these. Regroup as shown in number 9.

9. $\begin{array}{r} {\scriptstyle 11} \\ 435 \\ \times\ 3 \\ \hline 1{,}305 \end{array}$

10. $\begin{array}{r} 229 \\ \times\ 9 \\ \hline \end{array}$

11. $\begin{array}{r} 564 \\ \times\ 4 \\ \hline \end{array}$

12. $\begin{array}{r} 495 \\ \times\ 5 \\ \hline \end{array}$

13. $\begin{array}{r} 892 \\ \times\ 5 \\ \hline \end{array}$

14. $\begin{array}{r} 667 \\ \times\ 4 \\ \hline \end{array}$

15. $\begin{array}{r} 739 \\ \times\ 7 \\ \hline \end{array}$

16. $\begin{array}{r} 363 \\ \times\ 4 \\ \hline \end{array}$

Multiplication #47

Directions: Solve the problems.

1. 173 x 6	2. 227 x 3	3. 402 x 1
4. 420 x 1	5. 324 x 8	6. 172 x 4
7. 286 x 8	8. 509 x 4	9. 533 x 8
10. 388 x 1	11. 620 x 6	12. 662 x 3

Multiplication #48

Directions: Solve each multiplication problem. Use each answer's letter to discover a secret question and its answer.

1. 14 x 2 = **W**	**2.** 331 x 2 = **I**	**3.** 244 x 2 = **T**	**4.** 321 x 3 = **N**	**5.** 212 x 4 = **L**
6. 412 x 2 = **M**	**7.** 313 x 3 = **A**	**8.** 441 x 2 = **H**	**9.** 142 x 2 = **P**	**10.** 211 x 4 = **?**
11. 324 x 2 = **U**	**12.** 332 x 3 = **C**	**13.** 322 x 3 = **!**	**14.** 123 x 2 = **O**	**15.** 241 x 2 = **Y**

___ ___ ___   ___ ___ ___
28 882 246   996 939 963

___ ___ ___ ___ ___ ___ ___ ___ ___
824 648 848 488 662 284 848 482 844

___   ___ ___ ___ ___
662   996 939 963 966

Multiplication #49

Directions: Solve the problems.

1. 835 x 3	**2.** 152 x 7	**3.** 254 x 5
4. 851 x 1	**5.** 138 x 2	**6.** 417 x 8
7. 317 x 4	**8.** 458 x 7	**9.** 594 x 5
10. 180 x 4	**11.** 538 x 1	**12.** 728 x 6

Ready·Set·Learn

Multiplication #50

Directions: Solve these problems. The first two have been done for you.

1. 123 x 10 1,230	**2.** 543 x 10 5,430	**3.** 243 x 10	**4.** 341 x 10
5. 534 x 10	**6.** 333 x 10	**7.** 762 x 10	**8.** 300 x 10
9. 700 x 10	**10.** 900 x 10	**11.** 250 x 10	**12.** 460 x 10
13. 490 x 10	**14.** 474 x 10	**15.** 716 x 10	**16.** 642 x 10

Multiplication #51

Directions: Solve the problems. The first one has been done for you.

1. 5,132 x 5 = 25,660	**2.** 6,243 x 2	**3.** 8,761 x 4
4. 3,652 x 4	**5.** 3,491 x 2	**6.** 4,842 x 7
7. 6,766 x 3	**8.** 1,991 x 7	**9.** 2,864 x 9
10. 4,771 x 8	**11.** 2,664 x 5	**12.** 3,769 x 6

Ready·Set·Learn

Multiplication #52

Directions: Solve the problems. The first one has been done for you.

1.
```
  3,901
x     7
-------
 27,307
```

2.
```
  4,009
x     7
-------
```

3.
```
  6,008
x     7
-------
```

4.
```
  4,881
x     8
-------
```

5.
```
  8,888
x     9
-------
```

6.
```
  3,811
x     3
-------
```

7.
```
  2,345
x     5
-------
```

8.
```
  7,009
x     4
-------
```

9.
```
  6,439
x     7
-------
```

Multiplication #53

Directions: Solve these problems. The first on has been done for you.

1. 12 x 10 00 + 120 120	**2.** 14 x 22	**3.** 23 x 12	**4.** 31 x 24
5. 34 x 22	**6.** 22 x 32	**7.** 13 x 33	**8.** 20 x 57
9. 71 x 62	**10.** 43 x 31	**11.** 33 x 22	**12.** 41 x 43

Ready·Set·Learn

Multiplication #54

Directions: Solve the problems.

1. $\begin{array}{r} 974 \\ \times\ 46 \\ \hline \end{array}$	**2.** $\begin{array}{r} 889 \\ \times\ 75 \\ \hline \end{array}$	**3.** $\begin{array}{r} 771 \\ \times\ 43 \\ \hline \end{array}$
4. $\begin{array}{r} 809 \\ \times\ 48 \\ \hline \end{array}$	**5.** $\begin{array}{r} 907 \\ \times\ 28 \\ \hline \end{array}$	**6.** $\begin{array}{r} 706 \\ \times\ 76 \\ \hline \end{array}$
7. $\begin{array}{r} 322 \\ \times\ 16 \\ \hline \end{array}$	**8.** $\begin{array}{r} 444 \\ \times\ 28 \\ \hline \end{array}$	**9.** $\begin{array}{r} 512 \\ \times\ 41 \\ \hline \end{array}$

Multiplication #55

Directions: Solve each multiplication problem. Fill in the answer circle for your choice.

1.

$$\begin{array}{r} 49 \\ \times\ 34 \\ \hline \end{array}$$

Ⓐ 1,686 Ⓒ 1,666

Ⓑ 2,666 Ⓓ 1,696

2.

$$\begin{array}{r} 77 \\ \times\ 27 \\ \hline \end{array}$$

Ⓐ 2,079 Ⓒ 2,169

Ⓑ 2,179 Ⓓ 2,069

3.

$$\begin{array}{r} 88 \\ \times\ 37 \\ \hline \end{array}$$

Ⓐ 3,266 Ⓒ 3,156

Ⓑ 3,356 Ⓓ 3,256

4.

$$\begin{array}{r} 19 \\ \times\ 92 \\ \hline \end{array}$$

Ⓐ 2,748 Ⓒ 1,748

Ⓑ 1,758 Ⓓ 7,148

5.

$$\begin{array}{r} 87 \\ \times\ 55 \\ \hline \end{array}$$

Ⓐ 4,885 Ⓒ 4,795

Ⓑ 4,785 Ⓓ 4,985

6.

$$\begin{array}{r} 39 \\ \times\ 17 \\ \hline \end{array}$$

Ⓐ 1,663 Ⓒ 636

Ⓑ 663 Ⓓ 693

Multiplication #56

Directions: Solve each multiplication problem. Fill in the answer circle for your choice.

1. 17 x 28

Ⓐ 476 Ⓒ 4,076
Ⓑ 576 Ⓓ 478

2. 66 x 67

Ⓐ 4,322 Ⓒ 4,412
Ⓑ 4,422 Ⓓ 4,432

3. 19 x 57

Ⓐ 1,183 Ⓒ 1,193
Ⓑ 993 Ⓓ 1,083

4. 23 x 39

Ⓐ 997 Ⓒ 897
Ⓑ 987 Ⓓ 1,087

5. 47 x 26

Ⓐ 1,222 Ⓒ 2,222
Ⓑ 1,232 Ⓓ 3,222

6. 24 x 48

Ⓐ 1,154 Ⓒ 1,152
Ⓑ 1,352 Ⓓ 1,252

7. 94 x 49

Ⓐ 4,616 Ⓒ 4,606
Ⓑ 6,606 Ⓓ 4,660

8. 18 x 81

Ⓐ 1,438 Ⓒ 1,558
Ⓑ 1,448 Ⓓ 1,458

Answer Key

Page 4

1. 15
2. 12
3. 8
4. 24
5. 24
6. 27
7. 10
8. 18
9. 7
10. 35
11. 20
12. 15

Page 5

5. 2 groups of 2
6. 4 groups of 4

Page 6

1. 9; 3 x 3 = 9
2. 8; 2 x 4 = 8
3. 12; 3 x 4 = 12
4. 10; 2 x 5 = 10

Page 7

1. 5 x 4 = 20
2. 6 x 3 = 18
3. 2 x 6 = 12
4. 3 x 4 = 12

Page 8

1. 1
2. 4
3. 1
4. 8
5. 3
6. 2
7. 1
8. 1
9. 11

Page 9

1. 2
2. 8
3. 20
4. 4
5. 10
6. 22
7. 6
8. 12
9. 24
10. 14
11. 16
12. 18

Page 10

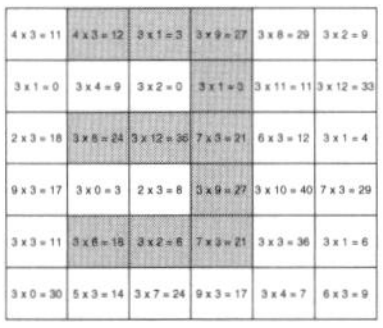

Page 11

1. 12
2. 18
3. 27

Page 13

clockwise, from upper left:

1. 0, 28, 48, 4
2. 44, 12, 24, 32
3. 8, 20, 40, 36
4. 4, 32, 28, 8

Page 14

1. 25
2. 35
3. 5
4. 10
5. 40

Bonus:
10 x 5 = 50

Page 15

1. 10
2. 5
3. 30
4. 55
5. 35
6. 50
7. 25
8. 50
9. 20
10. 45
11. 15
12. 40
13. 20
14. 55

Message: Can you multiply?

Page 16

1. 6
2. 10
3. 2
4. 4
5. 8
6. 14
7. 12
8. 18

Page 17

1. 6
2. 12
3. 24
4. 30
5. 18
6. 54
7. 36
8. 60
9. 48
10. 42

Page 18

1. 7
2. 14
3. 28
4. 35
5. 21
6. 63
7. 42
8. 70
9. 56
10. 42

Page 19

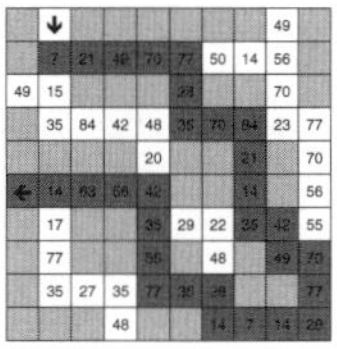

Page 20

1. 24
2. 16
3. 32
4. 40
5. 7
6. 70
7. 28
8. 12
9. 18
10. 30
11. 45
12. 0
13. 9
14. 18
15. 40
16. 60

Page 21

1. 4
2. 120
3. 28
4. 16
5. 27
6. 63
7. 0
8. 45
9. 72
10. 132
11. 21
12. 18
13. 30
14. 16
15. 81

Page 22

1. 5 x 3 = 15
2. 1 x 10 = 10
3. 4 x 2 = 8
4. 4 x 8 = 32
5. 2 x 7 = 14

Page 23

1. 10
2. 0
3. 3
4. 6
5. 5
6. 4
7. 8
8. 7
9. 1
10. 9
11. 2
12. 11

Page 24

1. 36
2. 42
3. 16
4. 0
5. 72
6. 56
7. 6
8. 24
9. 20
10. 24
11. 45
12. 64
13. 40
14. 21
15. 63
16. 56

Page 25

colored circles: 9, 18, 27, 36, 45, 54, 63, 72, 81, 90, 99, 108, 117, 126, 135

Answer Key (cont.)

Page 26

1. 5
2. 2
3. 4
4. 8
5. 10
6. 5
7. 6
8. 4
9. 10
10. 6
11. 9
12. 3
13. 9
14. 7
15. 6
16. 8
17. 4
18. 8
19. 9
20. 4
21. 10
22. 7
23. 6
24. 9
25. 7
26. 8
27. 4

Page 27

1. 42, 24, 12, 30, 18, 48, 36, 54
2. 49, 28, 14, 35, 21, 56, 42, 63
3. 56, 32, 16, 40, 24, 64, 48, 72
4. 63, 36, 18, 45, 27, 72, 54, 81

Page 28

1. 1, 2, 4
2. 1, 2, 3, 6
3. 1, 3, 9
4. 1, 2, 5, 10
5. 1, 3, 5, 15

Page 29

1. 24
2. 36
3. 36
4. 35
5. 54
6. 36
7. 24
8. 24
9. 81
10. 49
11. 42
12. 36
13. 72

Bonus: Woodrow Wilson

Page 30

Across

2. six
5. nine
6. twelve
7. fourteen

Down

1. sixteen
3. fifteen
4. zero
6. ten

Page 31

1. eight
2. twenty
3. thirty
4. eighteen
5. twelve
6. forty
7. nine
8. seventy
9. fifty
10. hundred

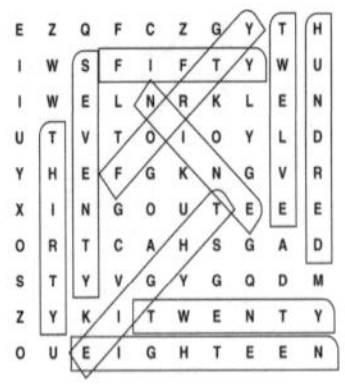

Page 32

1. 48
2. 42
3. C
4. 32
5. C

Page 33

1. 110
2. 120
3. 96
4. 132
5. 33
6. 99
7. 72
8. 120
9. 66
10. 48
11. 108
12. 88
13. 77
14. 36
15. 132
16. 84

Page 34

1. 13 x 6 = 78
2. 3 x 5 = 15
3. 13 x 8 = 104
4. 4 x 16 = 64
5. 17 x 3 = 51

Page 35

1. 48
2. 28
3. 39
4. 63
5. 88
6. 88
7. 68
8. 400
9. 108
10. 86
11. 99
12. 639
13. 630
14. 630
15. 300
16. 480

Page 36

Message: Shine like a star!

Page 37

1. 99
2. 30
3. 69
4. 246
5. 68
6. 75
7. 128
8. 125
9. 48
10. 110
11. 90
12. 135
13. 108
14. 220
15. 264
16. 132

Page 38

Across

4. 76
6. 134
8. 176
9. 365
11. 602
13. 474
15. 378
16. 588

Down

1. 774
2. 196
3. 31
5. 216
7. 320
8. 114
9. 368
10. 53
11. 680
12. 222
14. 45
17. 89

Page 39

1. 24
2. 24
3. 24
4. 36
5. 36
6. 36
7. 120
8. 120
9. 120
10. 105
11. 105
12. 105

Page 40

1. 252
2. 450
3. 651
4. 282
5. 760
6. 435
7. 237
8. 595
9. 603
10. 368
11. 702
12. 792
13. 456
14. 231
15. 57
16. 392

Page 41

1. 120
2. 320
3. 230
4. 110
5. 140
6. 330
7. 180
8. 200
9. 300
10. 700
11. 240
12. 310
13. 410
14. 440
15. 250
16. 370

Answer Key *(cont.)*

Page 42

1. 12 x 7 = 84
2. 1 x 3 = 3
3. 2 x 12 = 24
4. 3 x 10 = 30
5. 10 x 10 = 100

Page 43

1. 844; 4
2. 960; 9
3. 107; 7
4. 555; 5
5. 848; 8
6. 939; 9

Page 44

1. <
2. <
3. <
4. <
5. =
6. >

Page 45

1. >
2. <
3. <
4. =
5. <
6. >
7. <
8. =
9. >
10. >
11. 3 or lower
12. 6 or higher
13. 12 or lower
14. 4
15. 15 or higher

Page 46

1. 70
2. 72
3. 108
4. 180
5. 323
6. 143

Page 47

1. 9,999
2. 8,206
3. 1,261
4. 0
5. 8,488
6. 4,608
7. 7,108

Page 48

1. 848
2. 756
3. 258
4. 7,798
5. 918
6. 6,984
7. 963
8. 430

Page 49

1. 369
2. 428
3. 648
4. 696
5. 999
6. 1,284
7. 2,766
8. 2,496
9. 1,305
10. 2,061
11. 2,256
12. 2,475
13. 4,460
14. 2,668
15. 5,173
16. 1,452

Page 50

1. 1,038
2. 681
3. 402
4. 420
5. 2,592
6. 688
7. 2,288
8. 2,036
9. 4,264
10. 388
11. 3,720
12. 1,986

Page 51

1. 28
2. 662
3. 488
4. 963
5. 848
6. 824
7. 939
8. 882
9. 284
10. 844
11. 648
12. 996
13. 966
14. 246
15. 482

Message: Who can multiply? I can!

Page 52

1. 2,505
2. 1,064
3. 1,270
4. 851
5. 276
6. 3,336
7. 1,268
8. 3,206
9. 2,970
10. 720
11. 538
12. 4,368

Page 53

1. 1,230
2. 5,430
3. 2,430
4. 3,410
5. 5,340
6. 3,330
7. 7,620
8. 3,000
9. 7,000
10. 9,000
11. 2,500
12. 4,600
13. 4,900
14. 4,740
15. 7,160
16. 6,420

Page 54

1. 25,660
2. 12,486
3. 35,044
4. 14,608
5. 6,982
6. 33,894
7. 20,298
8. 13,937
9. 25,776
10. 38,168
11. 13,320
12. 22,614

Page 55

1. 27,307
2. 28,063
3. 42,056
4. 39,048
5. 79,992
6. 11,433
7. 11,725
8. 28,036
9. 45,073

Page 56

1. 120
2. 308
3. 276
4. 744
5. 748
6. 704
7. 429
8. 1,140
9. 4,402
10. 1,333
11. 726
12. 1,763

Page 57

1. 44,804
2. 66,675
3. 33,153
4. 38,832
5. 25,396
6. 53,656
7. 5,152
8. 12,432
9. 20,992

Page 58

1. C
2. A
3. D
4. C
5. B
6. B

Page 59

1. A
2. B
3. D
4. C
5. A
6. C
7. C
8. D

This Award Is Presented To

____

for

★ Doing Your Best

★ Trying Hard

★ Not Giving Up

★ Making a Great Effort